PAT CHAPMAN

Curries

Photography by SIMON WHEELER

THE MASTER CHEFS

TED SMART

PAT CHAPMAN's passion for curry was virtually inherited, his ancestors having been in India for 200 years.

He founded the world-renowned Curry Club in Surrey in 1982 and it was not long before he set up a national network of curry restaurant reporters, which led to his regular publishing of the highly successful *Good Curry Restaurant Guide*, with its prestigious awards to top restaurants.

Pat frequently broadcasts on television and radio, and holds regular cookery courses. He is often to be seen demonstrating at major food shows and stores. He is a consultant chef to a number of UK Indian restaurants and he has appeared as a guest chef for Hilton Hotels and Selfridges Restaurant in London, as well as at the celebrated Taj Mahal Intercontinental hotel in Bombay.

Pat is best known as a cookery author. His 18 books have sold approaching 1 million copies, and include such best sellers as *The Curry Club 250 Favourite Curries and Accompaniments*, *The Balti Curry Cookbook*, *Curry Club Indian Restaurant Cookbook* and *Quick and Easy Curries* for BBC Books. His repertoire also includes successful books on Thai, Chinese, Bangladeshi and Middle Eastern cookery.

Photograph by Chris Capstick

CONTENTS

CHICKEN TIKKA MASALA CURRY   8

PAKISTANI VEGETABLE BALTI   10

NORTH INDIAN KEEMA CURRY   12

BANGLADESHI CHICKEN REZALA   14

BOMBAY LAMB DHANSAK   16

COCHIN VEGETABLE CURRY   18

SRI LANKAN DUCK CURRY   20

THAI KING PRAWN RED CURRY   22

CHINESE PORK CURRY   24

CARIBBEAN PEPPER POT   26

THE BASICS   28
    PREPARING THE INGREDIENTS
    THE INITIAL FRY
    GARNISHING AND SERVING
    FREEZING
    SPECIALIST INGREDIENTS

Think of a word which alone
describes a single dish, a complete
meal, and the cuisine of a nation.
That word is curry, and no other
food word does that. But then there
is no other food better than curry.

INTRODUCTION

If we are not born to it, most of us first meet curry at a local restaurant. Many of us come to love the undisputed king of the British curry house – Chicken Tikka Masala. Indeed, as one of my favourites, it deserves its place in this book. The same can be said of Balti. Before long, though, we realise there's more to curry than restaurant favourites.

So for the remaining eight recipes, let's voyage to those places where people are lucky enough to enjoy curry as their staple food. I call them the curry lands. Under a tropical sun, balmy winds waft appetizing aromas from lush leaves and pods and seeds. In generations past, people plucked these spicy capsules and dared to add them to their food, creating tastes as tantalizing as the aromas. Each curry land has its distinctive flavours and many curries. Where to start and what to chose?

With great difficulty I selected these recipes as an introduction to the remarkable world of curry. They are as varied and as authentic as possible, yet they are really quite easy to prepare and cook, using readily available ingredients and spices. They're favourites of mine and I hope that, as you try them, they will become yours too. I'm sure you'll enjoy the adventure.

Pat Chapman

CHICKEN TIKKA MASALA CURRY

85 ML/3 FL OZ NATURAL YOGURT

2 TABLESPOONS TOMATO PURÉE

1 TABLESPOON PAPRIKA

½ TEASPOON CHILLI POWDER

675 G/1½ LB SKINLESS, BONELESS
CHICKEN BREAST, CUBED

4 TABLESPOONS VEGETABLE OIL

4 GARLIC CLOVES, FINELY CHOPPED

3 TABLESPOONS RED TANDOORI
PASTE

2 SMALL ONIONS, FINELY CHOPPED

½ RED PEPPER, FINELY CHOPPED

½ GREEN PEPPER, FINELY CHOPPED

4 CANNED PLUM TOMATOES,
CHOPPED

200 ML/7 FL OZ CANNED CREAM
OF TOMATO SOUP

85 ML/3 FL OZ SINGLE CREAM

2 TEASPOONS GARAM MASALA

2 TEASPOONS CHOPPED MANGO
CHUTNEY

1 TABLESPOON COCONUT MILK
POWDER

1 TABLESPOON FINELY CHOPPED
FRESH MINT

2 TABLESPOONS CHOPPED FRESH
CORIANDER LEAVES

SALT

SERVES 4

Mix the yogurt with the tomato
purée, paprika and chilli powder.
Mix in the chicken cubes to coat
them evenly.

Heat the oil in a wok or karahi
and carry out the initial fry
(page 29) with the garlic, tandoori
paste and onions.

Increase the heat, add the
peppers and stir briefly. Add the
chicken and all the yogurt mixture
and stir-fry for about 3 minutes.

Add the tomatoes and stir well.
Gradually add the tomato soup,
little by little over 5 minutes,
stirring often.

Add the cream, garam masala,
mango chutney, coconut powder,
mint and coriander and stir-fry for
a further 5–8 minutes or until the
chicken is cooked through. Season
to taste, garnish and serve.

PAKISTANI VEGETABLE BALTI

400 G/14 OZ CANNED CHICKPEAS
4 TABLESPOONS VEGETABLE OIL
4 GARLIC CLOVES, FINELY CHOPPED
2 SMALL ONIONS, SLICED
1 RED PEPPER, CHOPPED
½ YELLOW PEPPER, CHOPPED
2–3 GREEN CHILLIES, SLICED
  (OPTIONAL)
400 G/14 OZ SPINACH
150 G/5 OZ MUSHROOMS,
  QUARTERED
1 TABLESPOON TOMATO KETCHUP
6 CHERRY TOMATOES, HALVED
2 TEASPOONS CHOPPED MANGO
  CHUTNEY
1 TABLESPOON EACH OF CHOPPED
  FRESH MINT AND CORIANDER
  LEAVES
SALT

WHOLE SPICES

1 TEASPOON CORIANDER SEEDS
½ TEASPOON EACH OF CUMIN SEEDS
  AND FENNEL SEEDS
6 WHOLE GREEN CARDAMOM PODS

GROUND SPICES

2 TEASPOONS DRIED FENUGREEK
  LEAVES★
½ TEASPOON EACH OF BLACK
  PEPPER, TURMERIC AND CLOVES
⅓ TEASPOON CINNAMON

SERVES 4

Heat a wok or karahi over fairly high heat, adding no oil. Add the whole spices and dry-fry, stirring constantly, for about 30 seconds. Leave to cool, then grind in a coffee grinder. Add the ground spices and mix well. Drain the can of chickpeas, reserving the liquid.

Heat the oil in a wok or karahi and carry out the initial fry (page 29) with the garlic, spices and onions.

Increase the heat and add the peppers and chillies, if using. Stir-fry for about 3 minutes.

Add the spinach and some of the chickpea liquid and stir-fry for a further 2–3 minutes. Add the chickpeas, the remaining liquid and all the remaining ingredients, except the salt.

Add just enough water to create the desired gravy consistency and stir-fry for 2–3 minutes or until well mixed and hot through. Season to taste, garnish and serve.

NORTH INDIAN KEEMA CURRY

4 TABLESPOONS CORN OIL

2–3 GARLIC CLOVES, FINELY
CHOPPED

2.5 CM/1 INCH CUBE OF FRESH
GINGER, CHOPPED

2 ONIONS, SLICED

600 G/1¼ LB LEAN MINCED
BEEF, LAMB OR PORK

½ RED PEPPER, SLICED

1–2 GREEN CHILLIES, SLICED
(OPTIONAL)

3–4 BAY LEAVES

300 ML/10 FL OZ CANNED CREAM
OF TOMATO SOUP

6 CHERRY TOMATOES, HALVED

2 TEASPOONS GARAM MASALA

100 G/3½ OZ CANNED
SWEETCORN AND ITS LIQUID

1 TEASPOON SUGAR

1 TABLESPOON CHOPPED FRESH
CORIANDER LEAVES

SALT

GROUND SPICES

1 TEASPOON EACH OF CORIANDER
AND CUMIN

½ TEASPOON EACH OF PAPRIKA,
HOT CURRY POWDER AND
TURMERIC

⅓ TEASPOON EACH OF CINNAMON,
CLOVES AND MANGO POWDER
(AMCHOOR)★

SERVES 4

Preheat the oven to 190°C/375°F/
Gas Mark 5 and warm a 2.3–
2.8 litre/4–5 pint casserole dish.

Heat the oil in a wok or karahi
and carry out the initial fry
(page 29) with the garlic, ginger,
ground spices and onions.

Increase the heat and add the
mince, pepper, chillies, if using, and
bay leaves. Stir-fry until thoroughly
mixed, then transfer to the
casserole dish, cover and place in
the hot oven.

After 20 minutes, stir in half the
tomato soup.

After a further 20 minutes, stir
in all the remaining ingredients,
except the salt, and cook for a final
20 minutes. Season to taste, garnish
and serve.

BANGLADESHI CHICKEN REZALA

4 TABLESPOONS GHEE OR
   CLARIFIED BUTTER
4 GARLIC CLOVES, FINELY CHOPPED
2 ONIONS, FINELY CHOPPED
675 G/1½ LB SKINLESS, BONELESS
   CHICKEN BREAST, CUBED
2–3 GREEN CHILLIES, SLICED
   LENGTHWAYS (OPTIONAL)
200 ML/7 FL OZ EVAPORATED MILK
2 TABLESPOONS SULTANAS
   (OPTIONAL)
4 TEASPOONS GROUND ALMONDS
1 TABLESPOON COCONUT MILK
   POWDER
1 TEASPOON GRANULATED SUGAR
2 TABLESPOONS CHOPPED FRESH
   CORIANDER LEAVES
2 TEASPOONS CHOPPED FRESH MINT
20 SAFFRON STRANDS (OPTIONAL)
2 TEASPOONS GARAM MASALA
SALT

SPICES

1 TEASPOON CORIANDER SEEDS,
   CRUSHED
1 TEASPOON CUMIN SEEDS
½ TEASPOON EACH OF BLACK
   MUSTARD SEEDS, FENNEL SEEDS,
   SESAME SEEDS AND WILD ONION
   SEEDS (KALONJI)★
⅓ TEASPOON FENUGREEK SEEDS

SERVES 4

Heat the ghee or clarified butter in a wok or karahi and carry out the initial fry (page 29) with the garlic, spices and onions.

Increase the heat and add the chicken and chillies, if using. Stir-fry for about 3 minutes. As the ingredients start to sizzle, gradually add the evaporated milk, little by little over 5 minutes.

Reduce the heat to a simmer and add the sultanas, if using, ground almonds, coconut powder and sugar, and stir-fry for a further 5 minutes.

Add the coriander, mint, saffron, garam masala and just enough water to maintain a creamy consistency. Stir-fry for a further 5–8 minutes or until the chicken is cooked through. Season to taste, garnish and serve.

BOMBAY LAMB DHANSAK

125 G/4 OZ SPLIT RED LENTILS,
   SOAKED FOR 20 MINUTES
4 TABLESPOONS VEGETABLE OIL
4 GARLIC CLOVES, FINELY CHOPPED
2 SMALL ONIONS, SLICED
450 G/1 LB LEG OF LAMB, CUBED
1 LARGE POTATO, QUARTERED
2–3 BAY LEAVES
400 G/14 OZ CANNED RATATOUILLE
1 TEASPOON DRIED FENUGREEK
   LEAVES ★
1 TABLESPOON COCONUT MILK
   POWDER
1 TEASPOON GARAM MASALA
1 TABLESPOON CLEAR HONEY
1 TABLESPOON CHOPPED FRESH MINT
1 TABLESPOON CHOPPED FRESH
   CORIANDER LEAVES
SALT

WHOLE SPICES

1 TABLESPOON CORIANDER SEEDS
½ TEASPOON CUMIN SEEDS
3 WHOLE BROWN CARDAMOM PODS
4 WHOLE GREEN CARDAMOM PODS
2 WHOLE STAR ANISE PODS

GROUND SPICES

½ TEASPOON EACH OF CINNAMON,
   NUTMEG, TURMERIC AND CHILLI
   POWDER

SERVES 4

Heat a wok or karahi over fairly
high heat. Add the whole spices
and dry-fry, stirring constantly, for
about 30 seconds. Leave to cool,
then grind in a coffee grinder. Add
the ground spices and mix well.

Bring 300 ml/½ pint water to
the boil. Rinse the lentils, add to
the water; simmer for 20 minutes.

Preheat the oven to 190°C/
375°F/Gas Mark 5; warm a 2.3–
2.8 litre/4–5 pint casserole dish.

Heat the oil in a wok or karahi
and carry out the initial fry (page 29)
with the garlic, spices and onions.

Increase the heat, add the lamb
and potato and stir-fry until mixed.
Transfer to the casserole dish, cover
and place in the hot oven.

After 20 minutes, stir in the bay
leaves, ratatouille and lentils.

After a further 20 minutes, stir
in all the remaining ingredients,
except the salt. Add a little water if
the mixture looks dry.

Cook for a final 20 minutes, then
test the lamb for tenderness (if
necessary, return to the oven until
the lamb is tender). Season to taste,
garnish and serve.

COCHIN VEGETABLE CURRY

125 G/4 OZ NEW POTATOES,
  HALVED
125 G/4 OZ CANNED RED KIDNEY
  BEANS
4 TABLESPOONS SUNFLOWER OIL
2 GARLIC CLOVES, SLICED
1 SMALL RED ONION, SLICED
2–4 FRESH RED CHILLIES, CHOPPED
  (OPTIONAL)
125 G/4 OZ GREEN BEANS, TOPPED
  AND TAILED
½ AUBERGINE, DICED
2 SMALL CARROTS, DICED
10–12 DRIED OR FRESH CURRY
  LEAVES★
300 ML/10 FL OZ NATURAL
  YOGURT
1 TABLESPOON CHOPPED FRESH
  CORIANDER LEAVES
SALT

SPICES

1 TEASPOON EACH OF BLACK
  MUSTARD SEEDS AND
  SESAME SEEDS
½ TEASPOON EACH OF CRUSHED
  BLACK PEPPERCORNS AND
  TURMERIC
⅓ TEASPOON CHOPPED DRIED
  RED CHILLIES

SERVES 4

Boil the potatoes until tender.
Drain and rinse the kidney beans.

Heat the oil in a wok or karahi
and carry out the initial fry
(page 29) with the garlic, spices
and onion.

Add the chillies, if using, beans,
aubergine and carrots, and stir-fry
for about 3 minutes.

Gradually add the curry leaves
and yogurt, little by little over 5
minutes, stirring frequently and
ensuring that the mixture simmers
but does not boil.

Add the potatoes and coriander
leaves and simmer for a further 4–5
minutes or until hot through.
Season to taste, garnish and serve.

SRI LANKAN DUCK CURRY

675 G/1½ LB SKINLESS, BONELESS
  DUCK, CUBED
50 G/2 OZ CORNFLOUR
4 TABLESPOONS VEGETABLE OIL
3 GARLIC CLOVES, FINELY CHOPPED
2.5 CM/1 INCH CUBE OF FRESH
  GINGER, FINELY CHOPPED
2 ONIONS, FINELY CHOPPED
300 ML/10 FL OZ COCONUT MILK
1 TABLESPOON VINEGAR
1 TEASPOON WORCESTERSHIRE
  SAUCE
1 TABLESPOON MOLASSES OR
  MUSCOVADO SUGAR
1 TABLESPOON EACH OF CHOPPED
  FRESH BASIL AND CORIANDER
  LEAVES
1 TEASPOON GARAM MASALA
1–3 FRESH RED CHILLIES, SLICED
SALT

WHOLE SPICES

3 TEASPOONS CORIANDER SEEDS
1 TEASPOON EACH OF CUMIN
  SEEDS, FENNEL SEEDS AND BLACK
  MUSTARD SEEDS
6 WHOLE GREEN CARDAMOM PODS

GROUND SPICES

1 TEASPOON CINNAMON
½ TEASPOON CLOVES
⅓ TEASPOON CHILLI POWDER

SERVES 4

Heat a wok or karahi over fairly
high heat. Add the whole spices
and dry-fry, stirring constantly, for
about 30 seconds. Leave to cool,
then grind in a coffee grinder. Add
the ground spices and mix well.

Toss the duck in the cornflour
until evenly coated.

Heat the oil in a wok or karahi
and carry out the initial fry (page
29) with the garlic, ginger, spices
and onions.

Increase the heat and add the
duck. Stir-fry for about 5 minutes,
adding just enough water to keep
the duck moist.

Cook for a further 10 minutes,
stirring and adding a little water
from time to time.

Add the coconut milk, vinegar,
Worcestershire sauce and sugar and
mix well. Cook for a further 5
minutes, stirring from time to time.
Add the basil, coriander, garam
masala and chillies and cook for a
final 5–8 minutes or until the duck
is tender. The curry should be
creamy and not too thin. Season to
taste, garnish and serve.

THAI KING PRAWN RED CURRY

2–3 LEMONGRASS STALKS
4 TABLESPOONS SUNFLOWER OIL
4 GARLIC CLOVES, SLICED
5 CM/2 INCH CUBE OF FRESH
    GINGER, SHREDDED
4–6 SPRING ONIONS, CHOPPED
600 G/1¼ LB UNCOOKED KING
    PRAWNS, SHELLED, DEVEINED
    AND WASHED
1 TABLESPOON TOMATO PURÉE
1 RED PEPPER, CHOPPED
1–3 FRESH RED CHILLIES, VERY
    FINELY CHOPPED
3–4 KAFFIR LIME★ LEAVES
200 ML/7 FL OZ COCONUT MILK
100 G/3½ OZ BEANSPROUTS
12–15 FRESH BASIL LEAVES,
    CHOPPED
1 TEASPOON FISH SAUCE★ OR SOY
    SAUCE
SALT
2 LIMES OR LEMONS, HALVED

SPICES

2 TEASPOONS PAPRIKA
½ TEASPOON EACH OF CHILLI
    POWDER AND CHINESE
    FIVE-SPICE POWDER★

SERVES 4

Slit the lemongrass stalks lengthways, keeping each stalk in one piece.

Heat the oil in a wok or karahi and carry out the initial fry (see page 29) with the garlic, ginger, spices and spring onions.

Increase the heat and add the lemongrass, prawns, tomato purée, red pepper and chillies. Stir-fry for 5 minutes, adding just enough water to keep the prawns moist.

Add the lime leaves and the coconut milk, and reduce the heat to maintain a gentle simmer for 5 minutes, stirring occasionally.

Add the beansprouts, basil, fish or soy sauce and enough water to create a thin rather than creamy sauce. Stir to mix, and simmer for a further 1–2 minutes.

Discard the lemongrass stalks, season to taste, garnish and serve with the lime or lemon halves for squeezing over the curry.

CHINESE PORK CURRY

600 G/1¼ LB LEAN PORK, CUBED
50 G/2 OZ CORNFLOUR
4 TABLESPOONS GHEE OR
   CLARIFIED BUTTER
4 GARLIC CLOVES, SLICED
4 CM/1½ INCH CUBE OF FRESH
   GINGER, SLICED
1 TABLESPOON HOT CURRY
   POWDER
2 TEASPOONS CHINESE FIVE-SPICE
   POWDER★
2 ONIONS, SLICED
300 ML/½ PINT CHICKEN STOCK
   OR WATER
4 BAY LEAVES
225 G/8 OZ CANNED PINEAPPLE
   CHUNKS IN NATURAL JUICE
125 G/4 OZ OYSTER MUSHROOMS,
   SLICED
125 ML/4 FL OZ CRÈME FRAÎCHE
SALT

SERVES 4

Preheat the oven to 190°C/375°F/ Gas Mark 5 and warm a 2.3– 2.8 litre/4–5 pint casserole dish.

Toss the pork in the cornflour until evenly coated.

Heat the ghee or butter in a wok or karahi and carry out the initial fry (page 29) with the garlic, ginger, curry and five-spice powders and onions.

Increase the heat and add the pork. Stir-fry for about 5 minutes, adding just enough of the stock or water to keep the pork moist.

Add the bay leaves and the remaining stock or water, then transfer the mixture to the casserole dish, cover and place in the hot oven.

After 20 minutes, stir in the pineapple and juice.

After a further 20 minutes, stir in the mushrooms and crème fraîche. Cook for a final 20 minutes, then test the pork for tenderness (if necessary, return to the oven until the pork is tender). Season to taste, garnish and serve.

CARIBBEAN PEPPER POT

4 TABLESPOONS VEGETABLE OIL

6 GARLIC CLOVES, CHOPPED

3 ONIONS, SLICED

500 G/1 LB 2 OZ LAMB, CUBED

1 SWEET POTATO, CUBED

300 ML/½ PINT STOCK OR WATER

3–4 BAY LEAVES

1–3 FRESH RED CHILLIES, SLICED

1 GREEN PEPPER, SLICED

1 TEASPOON EACH OF BLACK AND
GREEN PEPPERCORNS

3 TABLESPOONS CHOPPED SUN-
DRIED TOMATOES IN OIL

125 G/4 OZ CANNED PINEAPPLE
CHUNKS IN NATURAL JUICE

2 TEASPOONS MOLASSES OR
MUSCOVADO SUGAR

1 TABLESPOON RED WINE VINEGAR

50 ML/2 FL OZ RUM

SALT

WHOLE SPICES

6 WHOLE GREEN CARDAMOM PODS

2 TEASPOONS FENNEL SEEDS

10 WHOLE CLOVES

5 CM/2 INCH PIECE OF CASSIA BARK

4 WHOLE STAR ANISE PODS

GROUND SPICES

½ TEASPOON EACH OF CORIANDER,
TURMERIC, PAPRIKA, GINGER,
CUMIN AND GARAM MASALA

SERVES 4

Preheat the oven to 190°C/375°F/
Gas Mark 5 and warm a 2.3–
2.8 litre/4–5 pint casserole dish.

Heat the oil in a wok or karahi
and carry out the initial fry (page
29) with the whole spices, garlic,
ground spices and onion.

Increase the heat and add the
meat, sweet potato and the stock or
water. Mix well, then transfer to the
casserole dish, cover and place in
the hot oven.

After 20 minutes, stir in the bay
leaves, chillies, pepper, peppercorns
and tomatoes.

After a further 20 minutes, stir
in all the remaining ingredients,
except the salt. Cook for a final 20
minutes, then test the meat for
tenderness (if necessary, return to
the oven until tender). Season to
taste, garnish and serve.

THE BASICS

Each of the recipes specifies its main ingredient – Dhansak, for example, is traditionally made from lamb. However, there is no reason why you can't interchange ingredients.

All ten recipes could be made from meat, but you would have to use the casserole method (described in the recipe for Keema Curry). Meat requires an average cooking time of 1 hour. For best results, with the least amount of stirring, cook the meat in a casserole dish of at least 2.3–2.8 litres/4–5 pints, with a tight-fitting lid.

Equally, you could use chicken, fish, shellfish or vegetables in any of the recipes, using the stir-fry method described under Chicken Tikka Masala Curry. A 30 cm/12 inch wok or karahi (an Indian two-handled wok) gives the best results. Thus all the recipes can be adapted for vegetarians.

Each recipe serves 4, and requires around 675 g/1½ lb of the main ingredient, weighed after preparation. The recipes can cooked for two people by halving all ingredients, but keep the same cooking time.

PREPARING THE INGREDIENTS

Meat should be trimmed of veins, gristle and most fat, and should be cut into approximately 2.5 cm/1 inch cubes.

Poultry should be skinned, off the bone and cut into approximately 4 cm/1½ inch cubes. Breast or leg is ideal.

Fish should be skinned, all bones removed, and cut into 4 cm/1½ inch cubes. Shellfish should be raw, shelled, deveined and washed.

Vegetables should be trimmed and washed, then cut into similar-sized pieces, so that they take the same time to cook and are easy to eat.

THE INITIAL FRY

To maximize flavours, curries require an initial stir-fry of the 'holy trinity' of the curry lands: spices, garlic and onion (sometimes a fourth is added – ginger). This initial fry removes raw and bitter tastes from the spices and, as the garlic, onion and ginger turn golden brown, they 'caramelize' (i.e. they become sweet in taste), and the ingredients become integrated. This is the most important technique in the whole curry cooking process and, as it is used in all ten recipes, I give it in detail here.

1 Heat the oil or ghee in a wok or karahi until hot, but well below smoking point.
2 If whole spices are being fried, add to the oil or ghee and briskly stir-fry for about 30 seconds.
3 Add the garlic (and ginger, if specified) and continue to stir-fry briskly for a further 30 seconds.
4 Add the ground spices (if used), stir briskly, then add the onion, and mix in well.
5 Keeping the heat high at first, stir-fry until the onion caramelizes. This will take between 10 and 15 minutes, depending on the degree of caramelization required, and the heat will need to be lowered progressively during this time. From time to time you may need to add a little water to keep things mobile.

GARNISHING AND SERVING

All curries benefit from a garnish in a contrasting colour. The photographs show some ideas, and I would suggest red or green chillies, left whole or cut into thin strips or slices, toasted flaked almonds, roughly chopped pistachio nuts, desiccated or flaked coconut, fresh coriander or mint leaves, chopped chives or spring onions,and swirls of cream or yogurt sprinkled with garam masala or paprika.

Curry is traditionally served with boiled or steamed rice or with Indian bread. Side dishes of fruity chutneys, tangy pickles and mild raitas (yogurt sauces) can be added according to personal taste.

FREEZING

Meat, poultry, fish and shellfish curries freeze and reheat satisfactorily. Generally, vegetable curries do not.

SPECIALIST INGREDIENTS

Most of the spices and specialist ingredients used in these recipes are readily available at supermarkets or delicatessens. A few, marked *, although distinctive in the particular recipe, are harder to find and can be omitted.

If you are having difficulty obtaining spices or specialist ingredients in the UK, please write, enclosing a stamped, self-addressed envelope, to: Pat Chapman, PO Box 7, Haslemere, Surrey GU27 1EP.

THE MASTER CHEFS

SOUPS
ARABELLA BOXER

MEZE, TAPAS AND ANTIPASTI
AGLAIA KREMEZI

PASTA SAUCES
GORDON RAMSAY

RISOTTO
MICHELE SCICOLONE

SALADS
CLARE CONNERY

MEDITERRANEAN
ANTONY WORRALL THOMPSON

VEGETABLES
PAUL GAYLER

LUNCHES
ALASTAIR LITTLE

COOKING FOR TWO
RICHARD OLNEY

FISH
RICK STEIN

CHICKEN
BRUNO LOUBET

SUPPERS
VALENTINA HARRIS

THE MAIN COURSE
ROGER VERGÉ

ROASTS
JANEEN SARLIN

WILD FOOD
ROWLEY LEIGH

PACIFIC
JILL DUPLEIX

CURRIES
PAT CHAPMAN

HOT AND SPICY
PAUL AND JEANNE RANKIN

THAI
JACKI PASSMORE

CHINESE
YAN-KIT SO

VEGETARIAN
KAREN LEE

DESSERTS
MICHEL ROUX

CAKES
CAROLE WALTER

COOKIES
ELINOR KLIVANS

THE MASTER CHEFS

This edition produced for The Book People Ltd,

Hall Wood Avenue, Haydock, St Helens WA11 9UL

First published in 1996 by

WEIDENFELD & NICOLSON

THE ORION PUBLISHING GROUP

ORION HOUSE

5 UPPER ST MARTIN'S LANE

LONDON WC2H 9EA

British Library Cataloguing-in-Publication data
A catalogue record for this book is available
from the British Library.

ISBN 0 297 83642 0

DESIGNED BY THE SENATE
EDITOR MAGGIE RAMSAY
FOOD STYLIST JOY DAVIES